Original title:
Space: The Pun Frontier

Copyright © 2025 Creative Arts Management OÜ
All rights reserved.

Author: Finn Donovan
ISBN HARDBACK: 978-1-80567-838-0
ISBN PAPERBACK: 978-1-80567-959-2

Eclipsed by Laughter

When shadows dance on the moon's face,
The stars giggle in a comic chase.
A comet slips on banana peels,
In the dark, it's laughter that heals.

Aliens joke about Earth's strange ways,
Their punchlines echo through cosmic bays.
Black holes chuckle, they can't resist,
As they gobble up each pun-filled twist.

Nova of Nonsense

A supernova bursts with silly cheer,
Creating giggles we all hold dear.
Galaxies swirl in a ticklish cheer,
Cosmic gags are what we all revere.

Puppy stars wag their tails in delight,
Drawing giggles in the velvet night.
Meteor showers with tickles galore,
Leave us laughing, begging for more.

Cosmic Jests

Asteroids hurl wisecracks in flight,
Remarking on the Earthling plight.
With every orbit, the humor grows,
As stardust tickles our human toes.

Jupiter roars with a jovial sound,
While Saturn's rings spin jokes all around.
The universe bursts with witty bars,
Shooting smiles like funny shooting stars.

Celestial Puns

A galaxy spins with puns so slick,
Astro-nerds laugh with every quirk.
Planets joke in their quirky orbits,
Their punchlines launch like shooting star bits.

Lunar laughter fills the starry plains,
Witty rhymes rocket through cosmic lanes.
In the vastness, joy is our guide,
As we float through humor, far and wide.

Galactic Giggles

In the cosmos, stars make jokes,
Witty comets dropping puns like blokes.
Planets spinning with a merry grin,
While black holes laugh, pulling all in.

Aliens chuckle, with tentacles they tease,
Shooting stars throw shade among the trees.
Nebulas burst, with colors that play,
Creating laughter, in a bright display.

Stardust Wit

Saturn's rings are quite the show,
They say they're jewelry, but where did it go?
Mercury's quick, never runs out of time,
Always zipping around, a nimble little rhyme.

In the asteroid belt, the jokes fly thick,
One hit a rock, and it laughed at the sick.
A lunar rover rolls, with wheels full of puns,
On the moon's surface, oh the fun never shuns!

Quantum Quips

Electrons dance, a charged little crew,
They bounce around, saying, 'What's up with you?'
Entangled humor, in pairs they confine,
One joke here, the other's on a line.

Heisenberg's party is quite the mix,
If you find the fun, you're lost in the fix.
Protons walk in, all positive vibes,
While neutrons chill, just sharing their jibes.

Interstellar Irony

A black hole's feast, like cosmic pie,
Eating light years, oh me, oh my!
Supernovae boom, 'What a blast!', they scream,
While galaxies swirl in a glittering dream.

Time bends here, but laughter stays straight,
Old stars tell tales, while the young celebrate.
A universe full of quirks and glee,
Let's toast with starlight, let's all just be free!

Nebula Nonsense

Stars twinkle like they lost their balance,
Gravity's a prankster in this cosmic dance.
Planets spin in a groove so absurd,
Alien DJs drop beats, have you heard?

Wormholes whirl, a delightfully wild ride,
Listen to cosmic jokes that won't be denied.
Quasars crack up with a blinding light,
Interstellar chuckles in the dark of night.

Astro Amusements

Saturn's rings spin like a circus show,
Eclipsing our worries, putting on a glow.
Jupiter's storms are just comedy acts,
Thunderous laughter from the gas giant packs.

Meteor showers bring a wild light display,
Wish on a comet, make your day gay.
Aliens giggle as they zoom on by,
Sending silly selfies through the cosmic sky.

Lunar Laughs

Moonbeams chuckle, lighting up the night,
Tides can't help but giggle in delight.
Craters whisper jokes from long ago,
Where do jokes come from? The moon won't show!

Rovers tripping on lunar dust delight,
Bouncing back up, ready for a fight.
Astronauts in space suits full of glee,
Craving a laugh as they float by me.

Comet Capers

Comets racing by with tails full of cheer,
Zooming past planets, spreading good dear.
Celestial pranks in the cosmic flow,
Watch out for space clowns putting on a show!

Asteroids dodging like they're in a game,
Hiding behind moons, they'll never be tame.
Shooting stars weaving through the night air,
Making wishes while they dance without care.

Galactic Grins

In the cosmos where jokesters roam,
Stars twinkle bright, like laughter's home.
Asteroids chuckle as they drift along,
While comets compose their giggling song.

A black hole yawns, 'Why so serious, friend?'
It swallows jokes, but they never end.
Planets spin tales with a whimsical flair,
As aliens chuckle without any care.

Quantum Quips

In the realm where photons play,
Light-speed humor brightens the day.
Atoms collide with a snicker and wink,
As particles dance on the edge of brink.

Waves travel far with a playful tease,
Echoing laughter on cosmic breeze.
Quantum cats giggle, they're never quite sure,
If they're here or there, but they always purr.

Celestial Comedy Club

In a club among the stars so wide,
Galaxies gather with giggles inside.
Martians tell tales of their interstellar ride,
While Saturn rings in with a punchline so fried.

Nebulas puff out a smoky jest,
Cosmic comedians all vying for the best.
Supernovae burst in roars of delight,
As laughter erupts on this stellar night.

Astro-Absurdities

Orbiting planets wear mismatched shoes,
Galactic travelers playing the blues.
An asteroid slips on a banana peel,
Spinning through space with a comedic zeal.

Gravity's pulling but jokes float away,
In this universe, everyone's play.
Twinkling stars wink, 'What's your best pun?'
In this cosmic dance, we all have our fun.

Black Hole Banter

In a universe filled with jest,
Black holes love a good roast,
They suck in all the great lines,
And then they leave you a ghost.

In the dark, they like to joke,
About how they can't find their way,
They always say, 'I'm not lost,
Just orbiting a little play.'

They pull in stars with charm and grace,
Then ask, 'Is this starry face too bright?'
Gravity makes them so profound,
But punchlines soar at the speed of light!

So if you drift near a void so deep,
Be ready to laugh, or take a dive,
For what's lost in space may find its way,
To a good quip that's sure to thrive.

Quasar Quirks

Quasars shine like cosmic jesters,
Flickering with a brilliant grin,
They tell tales of time and distance,
And how laughter can make you spin.

'How fast is light?' they often ask,
'Faster than your Wi-Fi, friend!
When I flicker, sparks do fly,
Just don't blink, it's quite the trend!'

Their giggles travel through the night,
In bursts of energy and cheer,
If stars had a comedy club,
Quasars would be the headliners here.

So hold on tight to your telescope,
When the show starts, don't fall asleep,
For the cosmos tells its funniest tales,
In winks of light, so pure and deep.

Comedic Constellations

In the sky, stars form quite the crew,
Orion whispers puns, it's true.
The Big Dipper pours out laughter,
As they share their tales—what joy they brew!

Cassiopeia strikes a pose so grand,
She says, 'Honey, don't you understand?
I'm a queen, but with a jokester's heart,
My wit can brighten any land!'

And down below, the Earthlings laugh,
While gazing at this starry scene,
Who knew the heavens held such fun,
In clusters with a playful sheen?

So let's all gather underneath the stars,
And share our jokes with the celestial might,
For the night sky hosts a comedic show,
That tickles our hearts till the morning light.

Pulsar Punchlines

Pulsars pulse with zest and zeal,
Tick-tock jokes that make you feel.
'Knock, knock!' they echo through the void,
The punchlines land like cosmic steel.

Every rotation brings a new delight,
A short burst of laughter, so bright.
'Why did the star break up with the moon?
It needed space, it took flight!'

With each beam that sweeps our way,
Pulsars bring their witty play.
They spin and twirl in joyful glee,
As they light up the night and sway.

So if you hear a rhythmic beat,
Join in the fun, don't miss a seat,
For the universe is a dance hall bright,
Where every punchline is a cosmic treat!

Quirky Quantum Queries

In a realm where particles dance,
They joke in waves, given the chance.
Entangled laughs across the vast,
Hilarity from futures cast.

Photons giggle in their flight,
As electrons play hide and seek at night.
With every quirk, they share a grin,
In the universe, mischief can spin.

The uncertainty principle reigns,
Where left is right, and right contains.
A comedic twist on laws so grand,
This cosmic joke is well planned.

So ponder deep on quarks and beams,
Let humor bubble in your dreams.
For in the atom's tiny core,
Laughter's what we're all searching for.

Exoplanet Exaggerations

Out past Mars, there's a planet blue,
With skies of pink, and rivers too.
Jupiter's moons wear hats so wide,
Orbiting around with cosmic pride.

Saturn's rings are made of cheese,
And Venus offers galactic teas.
While comets race in style so grand,
Meteor showers are an outdoor band.

Neptune sings with a voice so deep,
While aliens groove, they've lost the sheep.
A cosmic circus, wild and free,
Join the ride, come laugh with me!

So pack your bags and take a flight,
To worlds of humor, sheer delight.
Each exoplanet spins a tale,
With laughter riding every gale.

Stellar Snark

Oh sun, you think you're quite the star,
But I've seen your coronal flair from afar.
With plasma puns and heat that shines,
You roast the night with your bright designs.

White dwarfs crack jokes with nuclear glee,
While red giants feud—who's bigger, you see?
A supernova's a cosmic sneeze,
Sending humor flying like a breeze.

The black hole's wit is sharp and sly,
"Nothing escapes," they wink as they try.
Cosmic jests echo through the years,
Behind every laugh, there's stardust and tears.

So orbit around this snark-filled night,
Join the celestial smiles, oh what a sight!
For in this universe, both wild and vast,
A laugh is the joy that's meant to last.

Nebula Narratives

In a cloud of colors, bright and bold,
Nebulas paint stories yet untold.
Stars are born, with giggles and cheer,
In the stellar nursery, no need for fear.

They swirl and twirl like dancers in flight,
Bringing laughter to the cosmic night.
With tales of love and stellar pride,
These gas giants laugh, they won't hide.

A bubble nebula wears a playful grin,
While others puff clouds, just for the win.
Each flickering heartbeat is pure delight,
In the tales they tell through the shimmering light.

So drift among the stardust streams,
Where humor and dreams are more than it seems.
For in this vast, colorful plan,
Laughter's the language of every star's fan.

Lunar Laugh Lines

A green cheese moon hangs bright,
Makes me giggle with delight.
Alien cows jump and prance,
Moos from space, what a dance!

Stars twinkle with a wink,
Planets spin, pour a drink.
Astrologers lose their way,
Blame it on the Milky Way!

Comets fly with tails so long,
Singing out an endless song.
Rockets soar with zany grace,
Fuelled by laughs, they leave no trace!

Galactic gags that never quit,
Quasars joke, and black holes split.
In this cosmos full of cheer,
Laughter's echo rings so clear!

Asteroids of Amusement

Bouncing rocks with silly grins,
Orbiting like comical twins.
Crashing jokes upon a ride,
In a belt of chuckles wide.

Meteor showers of pure fun,
Silly antics never done.
Dodging giggles, swerving smiles,
Asteroids dance for miles and miles.

Zany planets join the game,
Filling space with endless fame.
Gravity holds them in a clasp,
While humor gives them quite the rasp!

Not a frown within their sight,
Comic stars ignite the night.
In this realm of joy we trot,
Laughter's thread cannot be caught!

Starry-Eyed Shenanigans

Twinkling stars in a bright parade,
Shooting laughs that never fade.
Galaxies burst with comic grace,
Cackling on in endless space.

Planets spin a wacky tale,
With giggles riding every gale.
Space-time jokes tethered with flair,
Lunar pranks fill the air!

Hyperdrive to humor's zone,
Launch a pun, then call it home.
Orbiting jokes, a cosmic race,
Every tick, a grinning face!

Wormholes lead to lands of jest,
In this verse, we're truly blessed.
Celestial chuckles far and near,
Bringing joy and loud cheer!

Black Hole of Buffoonery

Down the drain of laughs we go,
Spinning tales in the shadow's glow.
Gravity pulls, but we stay light,
In a whirl of endless delight.

Collecting giggles, oh so grand,
In a dark void where jokes expand.
Adventures brewed in cosmic stew,
Mirthful spirits shining through!

Silly slips into the abyss,
What a ride, we can't dismiss.
Gravitational pulls of fun,
A punchline race, we all can run.

So as we orbit round and round,
Find the humor lost, then found.
This black hole's the best retreat,
Where every funny face we meet!

Orbital Oddities

In a galaxy filled with strange sights,
Asteroids dance in their wild flight.
Planets giggle, spinning with glee,
While rockets chuckle, 'Is that a bee?'

A comet sneezes, 'A-choo!' it goes,
Moonbeams shine, tickling nose.
Aliens laugh over tea and scones,
Saying, 'Earthlings think they own the phones!'

Stars winking, playing hide and seek,
In the cosmic game, they all peek.
Black holes whisper, 'We're not so scary!'
Just a vacuum with dreams quite merry.

Galactic jests float in the dark,
Pulsars beep like a quirky lark.
With every giggle, the cosmos spins,
In this funny realm, everyone wins!

Cosmic Caricatures

Planets pose for a silly pic,
Each one trying a different trick.
Jupiter jests with giant flair,
While Saturn spins rings in mid-air.

Nebulae giggle, colors collide,
As dark matter takes them for a ride.
Galaxies twirl with a dramatic twist,
'What's the punchline?' asks a cosmic mist.

Shooting stars take a quick glance,
At comets parading in a silly dance.
Wormholes yawn, 'We're just a buzz,
Time's just a game, who cares? Just cause!'

In the void where laughter flows,
Stardust throws glitter like it knows.
Cosmic sketches, absurd and grand,
Creating a comedy no one planned!

Meteor Mischief

Meteors streak with a wink and grin,
Crashing the party, let the fun begin.
'Take that, Earth!' they giggle and dive,
Creating craters that seem alive.

Galactic gags bring bursts of light,
As stardust tickles the endless night.
What's that, a planet with a fuzzy hat?
No, it's just Mercury playing the brat!

Puns fly faster than sound in the void,
Where cosmic jokes are never devoid.
A supernova laughs, 'Watch me explode!'
While constellations form a funny code.

In the clutter of rocks that spin and jump,
The universe loves a playful thump.
With every crash, a chuckle rings,
Meteors share their comedic flings!

Starship Silliness

Starships zoom with giggles aboard,
Taking off like a cosmic sword.
'Watch out for traffic!' a pilot cries,
As they dodge space cows and winking pies.

Astro-goats munch on starlight hay,
As astronauts joke about their day.
'Who needs gravity?' they all cheer,
When floating in fun, there's nothing to fear.

Warp drives whir with a silly sound,
Through wormholes, laughter echoes around.
Galactic highways paved with glee,
Where even the asteroids dance with glee.

Hyperdrive hiccups, a funny mess,
As space-farers laugh in their comfy dress.
In the vastness where humor reigns,
Starship silliness forever gains!

Celestial Satires

In a galaxy not far away,
An alien tried stand-up on a hay.
He told a joke about stars in sight,
But they just twinkled and took flight.

A comet crashed into a moon,
Singing a tune, oh what a boon!
'Why did Mars break up with Venus?'
'Too much drama, lacking finesse!'

Astro Antics

An astronaut lost his favorite sock,
He searched each corner, each tick-tock.
It slipped behind a flowery nebula,
Said, 'I'm just being a little nebula!'

Saturn's rings had a fashion show,
Where moons strutted with flair, all aglow.
'Is it too much bling?' one meteor asked,
The judges laughed—what a cosmic task!

Orbiting Oddball Tales

A black hole opened a café,
Where all lost things would come to play.
'We serve gravity-defying treats,'
Said the chef with a spin—what feats!

One day, a star complained of the heat,
'I'm burning out—can I get a seat?'
The sun winked back, with a fiery grin,
'You'll be fine, just let the fun begin!'

Cosmic Comedy Showcase

A rocket ship told a funny tale,
Of aliens that danced like a whale.
They wobbled and bobbled—what a sight!
Even black holes giggled with delight.

A Martian quipped, 'I can't find my hat!'
His buddy replied, 'You look great like that!'
They rolled in laughter, so free and wild,
The universe smiled, just like a child.

Comedic Cosmoscape

In a galaxy not so far,
A comet tripped on its own star.
It laughed and spun, oh what a sight,
Chasing planets, dodging light.

Asteroids dance in a silly waltz,
Each one claims it has no faults.
They bounce and crash, a cosmic game,
In this bizarre, celestial fame.

A black hole jokes with a funny grin,
'Why are you so dense? Come on in!'
While stardust sparkles with twinkling glee,
As it tickles the moon and shouts, "Whee!"

So laugh among the stars tonight,
For humor shines like cosmic light.
In this vast expanse of jest,
The universe laughs, and we are blessed.

Nebula Narrators

In colorful clouds where whispers dwell,
A nebula spins its funny tale.
With gaseous puffs, it tells of fate,
'Why did the star never get a date?'

It floated high, a giggling mass,
Saying, 'My glow is made of sass!'
Light-years away, they all could hear,
The cosmic jest that brought good cheer.

Pulsars pulse in rhythmic beats,
Shaking with laughter that can't be beat.
Every burst a pun, so contagious,
In the void, they're outrageously outrageous.

So gather round, hear the light show,
As nebulae share their tales of woe.
In every cloud, a joke takes flight,
Comedy reigns in the galactic night.

Jovian Jestbook

In the shadow of a giant's grin,
Jupiter chuckles, where to begin?
'Why are moons so good at playing?'
'Because they know how to keep on swaying!'

With storms that dance and twirl about,
Each wild wind has a funny shout.
'If you think I'm big, just wait and see,
My belly's full of gas, whee!'

Saturn rings in, blaring its tune,
'Why do planets never play prunes?'
'They find them too hard to digest!
Cosmic fruits are much more blessed!'

Echoes of laughter swirl through the night,
Jovian jesters take their flight.
In every orbit, a punchline's spun,
The cosmos laughs, it's just begun.

Satellite Satire

Around the Earth, the satellites spin,
Spying on antics at a whirlwind's whim.
'Why don't they ever play hide-and-seek?'
'Because they always peek, so unique!'

They tweet their thoughts in bits and bytes,
While dodging meteors that give them frights.
'What do you call a star's disaster?
A flare up that's just a tad faster!'

Orbiting smiles with every rotation,
Humor spreads like wild elation.
'What's a satellite's favorite game?
A cosmic round of "Guess My Name!"'

So tune in close, don't miss the show,
As satellites share their comedy flow.
In every twist, a tale unfolds,
Entertainment from the heavens to behold.

Space-Time Chuckles

In a galaxy far with a punny twist,
Asteroids joke, you get the gist.
Planets giggle, stars they gleam,
Even black holes join the meme.

Comets race with a laugh so bright,
They leave behind trails of pure delight.
Alien jesters, cosmic jest,
Have a laugh, it's for the best.

Warp speed antics, on a light-year spree,
Gravitational pull? Just weigh it, you see.
An astronaut's shoes? They're out of this world,
With punchlines and laughter, the cosmos unfurled.

Saturn rings with jokes so bold,
In this universe, laughter's gold.
So hitch a ride on the humor ride,
Where each chuckle's a cosmic tide.

Cosmic Alliteration

Martian mice munch on moon pies,
Galactic giraffes gaze at the skies.
Witty wizards wielding weird wands,
Tickle the stars with laughter's bonds.

Quirky quarks quest with quirky quips,
Frolicking photons do funny flips.
Nebulae nod with knowing grins,
As cosmic clowns spin stellar fins.

Silly satellites spin in a circle,
Spouting spunky jokes that are sure to tickle.
Orbiting oddities, odes so light,
Making meteors burst, a dazzling sight.

Jovial journeys, jests in the void,
Humor ignites, never destroyed.
Shooting stars sizzle, slip and slide,
In the laughter of worlds where fun does abide.

Orbital Oratories

Singing stars serenade in sync,
While comets crash into cosmic ink.
Light-years of laughter, echoes loud,
Intergalactic giggles that astound.

Alien acrobats in a gravity-free show,
Flip and tumble, put on a glow.
Astrophysicists with punchlines anew,
Crafting humor in every view.

The Milky Way winks with playful cheer,
While Jupiter jests, drawing all near.
Black holes hoot as they play hide and seek,
In this stellar realm, each pun's unique.

Starry-eyed voyagers, brighten the night,
With tales of giggles, pure delight.
In the orbits of joy, we find our place,
Where jokes traverse the vastness of space.

Laughter Beyond Light

Beyond the stars, humor prevails,
With twinkly tales and comet trails.
Asteroids aim jokes at Earthly folks,
While the universe chuckles at cosmic blokes.

Eclipses hide giggles, shining through,
As planets whisper rumors too.
One sun's return, a hilarious twist,
Gravity drops, and none can resist.

Lunar laughs, like cheese on toast,
Galaxies gather, they seem engrossed.
Puns fly faster than the speed of light,
In the cosmic dance of sheer delight.

Countdown to laughter, five, four, three,
With humor's rocket, we all fly free.
So reach for the stars, don't lose your spark,
In this endless comedy, make your mark.

Infinite Innuendos

Planets in orbit, they swing and sway,
Stars whisper secrets, come out to play.
Gravity pulls, but so does the tease,
Asteroids joke while comets sneeze.

Galaxies giggle in a cosmic dance,
Nebulas twinkle, giving chance a chance.
Space pants were made for untold fun,
In this vast realm, laughs weigh a ton.

Aliens chuckle, with tentacles entwined,
Their humor's so bold, it's one of a kind.
Finding a pun in the sound of a quark,
They burst into laughter, igniting the dark.

Rocket ships zoom with a wink and a grin,
Engines of laughter, where jokes can begin.
Cosmic comedians, telling tales so bright,
Under the starlit sky, the humor takes flight.

Humor Beyond the Stars

Asteroids sit and tell cosmic jokes,
While Saturn's rings dance in sparkly smokes.
Mars rolls its eyes, in a planetary rave,
Each laugh echoing from crater to grave.

In the Milky Way, they all come to cheer,
Nebulae giggling, with nothing to fear.
Galactic puns float like dust in the air,
Even black holes can't help but share.

Hitchhikers roam with a wink in their eye,
Counting the stars and reaching for the pie.
The void may be vast, but the laughter is wide,
In the cosmic expanse, puns take a ride.

With supernovae bursting in bursts of delight,
Cosmic humor shines, oh so incredibly bright.
In this playful vastness, jokes never get old,
It's a universe of laughter, both young and bold.

Jupiters of Jest

On Jupiters' moons, the jesters abound,
With laughter so loud, it shakes up the ground.
Satellites spin tales that make gas giants blush,
In this jovial realm, there's never a hush.

Rings of laughter, encircle the sun,
Gravity's pull is just part of the fun.
Comedic collisions with meteors fly,
Where the punchlines land while the echoes comply.

Rocket boosters fire, taking off with a grin,
Far from the norm, where the wild jokes begin.
A cosmic jest as black as the night,
In every dark corner, there's always a light.

So beam us up, Scotty, to laughter we seek,
With endless punchlines navigation's peak.
In every quadrant, the humor expands,
As we soar through the cosmos, together we stand.

Lightyear Laugh Riot

Buzzing through orbits on laughter's own trail,
Faster than light, let the jokes set sail.
With galaxies laughing and stars having fun,
In this cosmic show, we're all number one.

Astrophysics fights, whose giggles are louder?
Neutron stars twinkle, not a single prouder.
Asteroids chuckle in a rocky refrain,
Cracking up comets till they're feeling the pain.

Warping through space on the punchline express,
Each twist and turn, just adds to the jest.
Zipping past planets with humor to spare,
Creating a riot, with laughter to share.

From quasars to pulsars, the jokes find their flow,
In this interstellar reality show.
No matter the distance, laughter's our light,
In this vast universe, let's party tonight!

Celestial Witty Whispers

Stars in the sky, they wink and grin,
Comets zoom by, they're off to win.
Planets make jokes, they spin and sway,
In the cosmos' chat, it's a pun-filled play.

Asteroids crack jokes, oh what a sight,
While moons pull pranks on planets at night.
Galaxies giggle, doing their dance,
In the universe's realm, who needs romance?

Intergalactic Giggles

Blasting off rockets, what a fun ride,
Aliens laugh, with arms open wide.
Meteor showers rain witty lines,
In the depths of the void, a humor that shines.

Quasars with punchlines explode in a flash,
While black holes swallow jokes with a crash.
Floating in orbit, the laughter spreads,
Tickling the stars and delighting our heads.

Cosmic Chuckles

In orbits of laughter, the planets collide,
Saturn's rings sparkle, with joy they confide.
Witty little aliens share tales on a beam,
Creating a universe stitched from a dream.

Pulsars are pulsing to a cosmic beat,
While space dust dances beneath our feet.
The nebulae giggle, they can't keep still,
As quantum quips echo, a cosmic thrill.

Nebulae of Humor

In a cloud of laughter, the cosmos unrolls,
With puns so bright, they capture our souls.
Planets tell stories, spinning their yarn,
Between shimmering stars, their humor is born.

A supernova bursts, with jokes to ignite,
While wormholes connect punchlines at night.
Floating through galaxies, enjoy the ride,
In the vastness of jest, let laughter abide.

Planetary Punslingers

On Mercury, they say, it's quite hot,
The sun's no joke, it gives quite a plot.
Venus is shady, a cloud of delight,
But try to see clearly? Oh, what a fright!

Earth has its quirks, like a cat and a dog,
While Mars just sits there, all dusty and fog.
Jupiter's storms are a wild, windy jest,
And Saturn's rings? A fashionable fest!

Uranus spins funny, it rolls on its side,
Neptune's just blue, like the ocean's pride.
The planets all laugh, making puns in the night,
In this cosmic arena, humor takes flight!

Galaxies giggle, in their swirling embrace,
A universe bursting, with laughter and grace.
Each star with its quip, shining bright in the dark,
In this vast cosmic dance, each pun leaves a mark!

Starstruck Satire

In the Milky Way's kitchen, a comet does bake,
It rolls out a pastry, oh, what a mistake!
Shooting for stars but the dough went aflame,
Now it's a crunchy, celestial claim to fame!

Black holes are drama queens, pulling you in,
Once you get close, it's all chaos and din.
They say they like parties, but you can't leave,
Their gravitational pull? Oh, who'd believe?

The moon tries stand-up, but jokes fall quite flat,
Like cheese in the sky — what a cosmic spat!
Stars often heckle, with that twinkling flair,
But really, they're shy; just too cool to share!

Planetary politics, oh, what a wild game,
With alliances formed just to lighten the name.
In this far-off comedy, laughter's the key,
As we orbit together, wild and carefree!

Lightyear Laugh Riot

Zooming through galaxies at hyper-fast speeds,
A lightyear's like running — just know the right deeds.
While asteroids laugh, tumbling here and there,
They dodge every punchline, without a care!

Quantum quips rise in a funny old haze,
Entangled with giggles that warp how you gaze.
Photons throw parties, they sparkle and bounce,
Though they can't find the time, they sure can pronounce!

Aliens joke in a language unknown,
In every lost signal, humor is sown.
They beam with a wink from their ships up above,
Sending puns light-years, like messages of love!

So let's spark a joke, across stellar seas,
With laughter that dances on cosmic degrees.
In this bright universe, let mirth take its flight,
As we chase down the fun, in the wild, starry night!

Comedic Cosmos

In the cosmos so vast, where the giggles ignite,
Stars gather for chuckles, under the night light.
What do you call a black hole that's funny?
A gravity joker, always hunting for money!

Saturn spins tales with rings full of jest,
"Uranus smells awful!" the planets invest.
While comets sail by, with tails full of glee,
They whisper old stories of space odyssey!

Nebulas swirl, in clouds of delight,
Creating new punchlines that dazzle the night.
Galactic puns linger, like echoes in time,
In the universe's laughter, we find our rhyme!

So raise up a toast with the stars all around,
In this infinite comedy, joy can be found.
Let's twinkle like stardust, with humor so bright,
In this comedic cosmos, we'll share our light!

Orbital Observations

In the sky, where jokes collide,
Stars giggle, they can't hide.
Moonbeams sparkle, humor flows,
Asteroids chuckle, who really knows?

Comets chase with tails that gleam,
Punchlines shot with cosmic beam.
Planets spin in laughter's whirl,
Jovial giants, just give them a twirl.

Galaxies swirl in rhythmic prance,
Laughter echoes, a cosmic dance.
Nebulas puff, light and bright,
Creating jokes that burst with light.

In this realm of starry fun,
You can't be serious, let's run!
Across the void, with giggles wide,
Cosmic laughter is our guide.

Comedic Cosmos Conundrum

Why do aliens love to tease?
They've mastered the art of freeze!
In the vacuum, their pranks take flight,
Tickling stars throughout the night.

Gravity? They say, 'What a bore!'
We float around, then drop and soar.
With each leap, hilarity grows,
As meteors crash with comic prose.

Quasars whisper a joke or two,
While black holes suck the humor, boo!
Yet in the void, laughter persists,
Eclipsing sense, it boldly twists.

The universe winks, a funny jest,
In this cosmic punchline quest.
Join the laughter, take your chance,
In the cosmos, we all dance!

Quantum Comedy Chronicles

In tiny realms where particles play,
Subatomic jokes come out to sway.
Electrons spin, tickling the air,
While photons wink without a care.

Entangled quips in a pithy draw,
If laughter's loud, it breaks the law.
Wave-particle humor intertwines,
Creating puns among the lines.

Bosons dance with grace and flair,
Creating gigs that float in midair.
Neutrinos sneer, they barely interact,
Yet their silence pulls the humor intact.

Each reaction bursts with comic zest,
In the quantum realm, we jest the best.
Embrace the quirks, take a leap,
In the chronicles where laughter creeps.

Zero-Gravity Gags

In zero-grav, the giggles soar,
Every joke floats, can't hit the floor.
With balloons of laughter in endless flight,
Tickled astronauts drift through the night.

Spacesuits wobble, a sight to see,
Their antics tickle the galaxy.
What's a rocket's favorite snack?
A comical boost, and that's a fact!

Falling stardust, they catch with glee,
Juggling humor like it's easy as can be.
Weighing laughter, cosmic and bold,
In the void, funny tales unfold.

Orbiting joy with a starry grin,
Every moment, a laugh to win.
In zero-grav, let your comic side beam,
Together we float, in laughter we dream.

Astro-naughty Whispers

In orbiting farce, we twist and we twirl,
Asteroids giggle, as stardust does swirl.
Alien mischief, with just a sly wink,
Your rocket's not hot, it just needs a drink!

Galaxies flirt in a cosmic embrace,
A comet sneezes—what a hilarious pace!
Astro-bunnies hopping from crater to crater,
Skip a light fantastic—laughter's the traitor!

Saturn's rings jingle with joyful delight,
While planets spin tales in the dead of the night.
Jupiter chuckles, "I'm larger, it's true,
But I'm still the one making gas jokes with you!"

So watch for the stars on a mischievous spree,
With cosmic giggles, they're wild and they're free.
From black hole to white dwarf, it's all in good fun,
In this bouncy universe, laughter's the sun!

Planetary Playfulness

Venus plays tricks with a sultry facade,
While Mars throws a party, way too overawed.
Neptune's got jokes, but they're deep in the sea,
As Uranus chuckles—'Guess who's laughing at me?'

Asteroids race in a silly space dash,
While constellations gather for a comedic clash.
Comets perform stand-up in orbits so wide,
Each punchline is meteoric, what a cosmic ride!

Solar flares sparkle with jokes that ignite,
As planets share puns in a galactic light.
When Saturn spins yarns, it's a dazzling show,
Get ready to laugh till you burst, here we go!

With laughter that echoes from star to bright star,
In this vast universe, we're never too far.
So buckle your seatbelt, enjoy the display,
In the great cosmic comedy, let's all seize the day!

Cosmic Corniness

Pluto may sulk, but he's still got a grin,
He tells us he's cute, oh what a spin!
Meteor showers drip with puns like confetti,
Each impact a giggle, the mood's feeling heady.

Black holes are sneaky, they suck up the light,
'Look, there goes a joke, oh what a sight!'
While stars twinkle brightly, with winks in their glow,
The cosmos is chuckling, putting on quite a show!

Asteroids tumble with flair and finesse,
Each collision brings laughter, but never distress.
In a vacuum of echoes, we hear cosmic glee,
From planets to meteors—let laughter run free!

Galactic giggles, oh what a delight,
So join the adventure, it's a star-studded night.
With quips that are stellar, and wittiness grand,
In this zany expanse, we're simply a band!

Milky Way Mirth

The Milky Way chuckles with stars in their arc,
Each twinkle's a punchline, a celestial spark.
Galaxies grin, with a spiral of fun,
And wormholes weave giggles like threads in the sun.

Cosmonauts laugh as they float through the void,
With quirks that are silly, no humor destroyed.
Puns travel fast on the solar wind's breeze,
While moons laugh together, putting minds at ease.

Space dust flutters like confetti in air,
Creating a party that's free of all care.
With a supernova's burst, the laughs multiply,
In the cosmos, we gather and let our joys fly!

So ponder that merry, magnificent sight,
Where giggles and wonders combine with delight.
In this boundless abyss, we find peace and mirth,
Together, we celebrate our comedy's birth!

Galaxy of Giggles

In a world where asteroids sing,
Planets wear hats and do their thing.
Stars twinkle with a winking eye,
While aliens dance and start to fly.

Comets streak past with a joke or two,
Meteor showers bring laughter anew.
Black holes are just shy of being polite,
They pull in the jokes, then vanish from sight.

Rockets blast off with a ticklish cheer,
Floating through humor, far and near.
Galaxies spin with a chuckle and grin,
In this cosmic realm, the fun's about to begin.

So grab your telescope, take a look,
Find the punchlines in the cosmic book.
With laughter as vast as the night sky,
Join the joyride, let's all fly high!

Spacetime Snickers

Warp drives whir with a giggling glee,
Time bends and twists just like three.
Quasars flicker with comic flair,
While wormholes tease, saying, "We dare!"

Lightyears seem like a joke well-timed,
As time travelers laugh, their spirits chimed.
Gravity pulls but can't hold the fun,
In this ticklish cosmos, we're all one.

Shooting stars throw jokes, oh what a sight,
Each twinkle a pun, oh so bright!
Gravity waves dance, a playful embrace,
In the fabric of humor, we find our place.

So join the laughter across the expanse,
As we spin through the cosmos in a fun little dance.
In this realm where punchlines bloom,
Even black holes are filled with a room of zoom!

Planetary Punchlines

Jupiter jests with his stormy frown,
While Saturn spins in a comical gown.
Mars giggles under its rosy hue,
With craters that chuckle, it's all too true.

Uranus winks, what a sly little star,
With rings of laughter that stretch afar.
Venus looks puzzled but laughs along,
In this playful world where we all belong.

Earth spins tales of a cosmic bank,
Where aliens giggle and thank the prank.
The Milky Way's lined with jokes untold,
Each star a spark in the laughter fold.

So bounce around in this cheerful scene,
With planetary mirth, so light and keen.
Grab a punchline, join the galactic flow,
In a universe of laughs, let lightheartedness grow!

Universal Uproar

In the void, where absurdity reigns,
Galactic puns flow through cosmic chains.
Supernovae burst with comedic flair,
Laughs echo through the twilight air.

Constellations map a humor so grand,
Each star a chuckle in this vast land.
Pulsars tick-tock with comic style,
They'll have you grinning all the while.

Asteroids roll with a humor so bold,
Cracking wise in their rocky hold.
From moons that tease to suns that beam,
In this wild universe, we all redeem.

So gather around for the cosmic play,
Where laughter sparkles, come what may.
In the uproar of worlds, come take a peek,
Join the fun—it's laughter we seek!

Starlit Shenanigans

Up in the sky, aliens glide,
They trip over stars, can't run, can't hide.
With each cosmic tumble, they giggle and roll,
Creating a ruckus, that's their main goal.

Saturn's rings are a hula hoop game,
Jupiter jumps in, the stars all exclaim.
As comets zip by with a whoosh and a cheer,
They dance in the darkness, their laughter we hear.

Meteor showers fall, oh what a sight,
They dodge and they weave, in the soft moonlight.
With each little splat, they chuckle and grin,
A slippery cosmos, let the fun begin!

So raise your space hats, enjoy the parade,
Where silliness reigns, in the intergalactic charade.
The universe beams with a mischievous spark,
In the realm of the stars, we all leave our mark.

Cosmic Caper Series

A rocket raccoon with a jetpack bling,
Floats past the sun on a golden swing.
He hiccups in zero-G, what a wild ride,
As planets roll over, laughter can't hide.

Bouncing on asteroids, they hold a contest,
To see who can jump and land with the best.
With each wonderful flop, they roll on the floor,
In a galaxy swirling with jokes and much more.

Galactic giggles echo in the void,
As puns fly around, none can avoid.
A black hole whispers, 'Come give me a try!',
But everyone knows it just wants a pie!

The stars all align for a pun-filled parade,
Where laughter sparkles as jokes cascade.
From rockets to robots, let the fun unfold,
In this cosmic caper, join us—be bold!

Nebula Nuttiness

In the heart of a nebula, colors collide,
A cloud of confusion where wits must abide.
Silly creatures dance with their rainbow hues,
Trading quips and puns like old friends would do.

Stars turn to giggles, planets to sighs,
As comets grow tails filled with wisecracks and lies.
A squirrel in a spacesuit floats by with a snack,
And winks with a nod as he spies a new track.

The void fills with laughter, absurdity reigns,
While rockets throw parties in cosmic terrains.
A telescope peaks over, finding the jest,
A galaxy's laughter, simply the best!

So come take a trip to this whimsical zone,
Where laughter's the language and absurdity's known.
In the dance of the cosmos, let silliness gleam,
For this nebula's nuttiness is all but a dream!

Lunar Laughter Lines

On a gibbous old moon, with craters so wide,
The critters of cosmos come out for a ride.
Hopping with joy in the silvery dust,
Bouncing to music, galaxies thrust.

A lunar llama spins with a dazzling flair,
While asteroids tumble without a care.
They've got a rock band playing tunes out of sight,
With syncopated rhythms, oh what a night!

The echoing giggles create quite the sound,
As Martians break-dance in circles around.
With every odd move, the stars start to shine,
In this quirk of the universe, everything's fine.

So gather your friends, let's all join the fun,
In this lighthearted realm where laughter is spun.
With meteors flaring and jokes on the line,
Come ride on the laughter of lunar design!

Cosmic Cauldron of Comedy

In orbits wide, the jokes collide,
A supernova of laughs, with humor as our guide.
Alien giggles float through the night,
While comets crack jokes at a meteoric height.

Galaxies swirl in a dance of delight,
Where moons tell tales that tickle the blight.
Asteroids poke fun at the paths they take,
In this cosmic cauldron, everyone's awake.

Black holes swallow punchlines whole,
But wormholes deliver, making laughter roll.
Quasars beam out the brightest of glee,
As stardust sprinkles joy on you and me.

In this vast void, we all join the fun,
Laughing at planets and each little sun.
It's a universe where humor's the key,
In this cosmic cauldron, let's all just be free!

Hilarious Horizons

Across the cosmos, laughter spreads wide,
With quirky aliens taking us for a ride.
They pull pranks as they spin and twirl,
On Saturn's rings, they give jokes a whirl.

Each starburst glimmers with giggles in tow,
Creating a rhythm, a cosmic show.
Nebulas swath in shades of delight,
From dusk till dawn, we dance through the night.

Mars throws a party with snacks made of dust,
Where rovers tell stories that are a must.
Venus joins in with a cheeky little sigh,
As confetti from comets flutters by.

Horizons laugh as they stretch and bend,
With humor so vast, it has no end.
Let's toast to the stars and their radiant beams,
In this universe, we all share dreams!

Pulsar Pranks

Pulsars flicker with mischief galore,
Telling tales of what happened before.
Each beep a giggle, each pulse a tease,
In this stellar playground, we all act with ease.

Light-years away, a prankster's delight,
A black hole's a vacuum that loves a good fight.
Gravity laughs, pulling jokes from the void,
In the jest of creation, we're all overjoyed.

Satellites spin like tops in a race,
Orbiting round with a smile on their face.
They hide behind planets, waiting to strike,
With funny little limericks that we all like.

In this cosmic circus, there's fun to be found,
As laughter echoes through the galaxies around.
Join the pulsar party, let humor ignite,
In the vastness of laughter, we all unite!

Starship Shenanigans

On a ship made of dreams, we sail through the stars,
With jokes that could rival the best of our bars.
A crew full of jesters, each one a delight,
Turning ordinary travel into a hilarious flight.

The captain cracks puns about cosmic cheese,
As meteors zip by with humor that frees.
Engines roar with laughter, the fuel of our joy,
When black holes admit they're just a ploy.

Gravity jokes keep us grounded and light,
As we reach for the heights, dancing through the night.
Starships collide in a giggling embrace,
In the comedy cosmos, we all find our place.

Navigating through starlight, we spark and we shine,
With laughter as fuel, our spirits entwine.
Join our zany voyage across the expanse,
In the realm of shenanigans, we all take a chance!

Milky Way Mockeries

In the cosmos, stars do twinkle,
But who knew they could also sprinkle?
Jokes light-years away from the norm,
Making black holes seem less forlorn.

Asteroids roll, they're a bit of a mess,
Crashing on planets, who could have guessed?
The sun's too hot, got no time for ice,
It cracks jokes, says it's always thrice nice.

Galaxies spin, they dance and they sway,
Even colliding, they have quite the play.
Comets with tails, a fashion display,
Showing off styles in their own fun way.

Nebulae giggle, their colors ablaze,
Creating new stars in a whimsical haze.
So let's laugh with the cosmos, let's all partake,
In the universe's jest, for all our sake.

Humor in the Heavens

Planets in orbit, taking their spins,
With moons that chuckle, where laughter begins.
Jupiter's giant, but what's his best joke?
It's all about gas, it gives quite a poke.

Saturn's rings, oh what a surprise,
Fashion statements that truly mesmerize.
Venus has secrets, but can't stop to share,
Too busy posing, with cosmic flair.

Stars throw a party, what a sight indeed,
But one gets too bright, they ask him to heed.
Constellations argue, which way do we meet?
They finally book tickets on comets for fleet.

Uranus just snickers, it's known as a clown,
While people giggle, never wear a frown.
The universe whispers, with jokes that delight,
In every corner, the laughter takes flight.

Celestial Comedy Gold

The sun wakes up with a radiant grin,
Giving the moon a playful spin.
Asteroids tease, they roll and they bounce,
While planets all chuckle, join in the flounce.

Mars comes in red, says, 'I'm quite the star,'
'But have you tried chocolate from a Martian bar?'
Earth rolls its eyes, sharing memes made of light,
While Saturn laughs hard, it's a dazzling sight.

Galactic puns fly like shooting stars,
As comets make wishes, they aim from afar.
Neptune gets splashed with a tidal jest,
While dreaming of laughter that never finds rest.

With black holes hiding their laughter inside,
Each voyage through heavens, pure joy we can't hide.
A universe full of humor and fun,
In this cosmic giggle, we all can run.

Stellar Stand-up

The stars gather 'round for a show in the night,
Sharing their tales, oh what a delight!
A meteor jokes, says, 'I'm falling for you!'
While planets respond with a cosmic woo-hoo!

The Milky Way snickers, a ribbon so bright,
It says, 'I'm the best, just look at my light!'
Black holes butt in, "We're full of surprise,
You're just dark matter, no need for disguise!"

Galaxy clusters chuckle, they're quite a crew,
Swirling together in a cosmic brew.
Distant quasars beam with laughter so bold,
In this universe, humor shines bright like gold.

So grab your stardust, let's float up high,
With laughter and joy, together we fly.
In this stellar stand-up, we'll never face doom,
With quips from the cosmos, we'll always have room.

Universe of Wit

In the cosmos where jokes collide,
Stars twinkle with puns, full of pride.
Asteroids laugh, they can't fall flat,
Gravity smiles; it's quite the chat.

Galaxies spin with a chuckle and cheer,
Nebulas giggle, 'We're hiding right here!'
A black hole says, 'You'll get sucked in!'
But all of us know, that's just a spin!

Planets parade in a jovial race,
They're searching for humor; it's a fun place.
Mars claimed he's the 'funny one,'
But Venus just laughed, 'Oh honey, not done!'

Laughter echoes in the void of night,
Quasars quip, 'Keep your jokes tight!'
So take a trip through this vast domain,
Where laughter and wit always reign.

Satellite Sarcasm

Orbiting laughter in perfect sync,
Moons mock, saying, 'Get off the brink!'
'Pluto's not a planet' they jest with glee,
But it still hangs out—you see, it's free!

A comet zooms by with a witty claim,
'Catch me if you can—I'm not to blame!'
Satellites wink, as they whirl around,
'We're the best in the galaxy; humor abound!'

Astro-puns fly just like meteor showers,
While aliens giggle, expending their powers.
'Why did Mars break with Venus?' they chant,
'Because there's no gravity in that romance plant!'

With every rotation, quips take the lead,
Space is a playground—come get a bead.
So strap in tightly; it's gonna be great,
In this orbit of jest, we all celebrate.

Milky Way Mischief

In the Milky Way's arms, chaos unfolds,
Stars prank each other; the stories are bold.
'Why's the sun always the center of fun?'
'Because without it, all jokes would be done!'

Asteroids bounce with a playful smack,
'They say I'm a rockstar, but I've got no track!'
Saturn rings in with a witty tone,
'With all this bling, I'm never alone!'

Each planet's a character, wearing their hats,
Mercury quips, 'I'm never late for chats!'
Jupiter boasts, 'I'm the king of the jest,'
While billions of stars join the fun-fueled fest!

So gather your laughs, make the trip today,
Milky moods warming, come join the play.
In this cosmic carnival, giggles will grow,
Believe in the mischief, let good vibes flow.

Cosmic Comedy Show

Gather round, folks, the show is about,
In a cosmic theater, laughter's what it's about.
Supernovae pop with a punchline or two,
And black holes pull laughter, like they do!

Galactic stand-ups take the stage with flair,
'Why's the astronaut a great chef? He can share!'
Crowds of comets roar, 'His dishes are stellar;
You gotta see him; he's quite a fella!'

Saturn's rings twirl in a graceful jest,
'Wanna see my bling? It's better than the rest!'
Each quasar lights up with a clever retort,
In this cosmic comedy, joy is the sport.

So next time you gaze at the night sky's glow,
Remember this laughter; let your own joy grow.
In the universe of humor, take your seat,
For the Cosmic Comedy Show, it's truly a treat!

Comet's Quip

A comet dashed past with glee,
'Thought I'd stop by for tea!'
With a tail that sparkled bright,
Sipping stardust, what a sight!

Asteroids chuckled on the side,
'He crashed our party, what a ride!'
While planets spun in their orbit,
Each shared a laugh, so don't forget!

The nebula giggled, swirling round,
'Who let the black holes stick around?'
With cosmic puns that filled the night,
Their humor not a meteorite!

As the milky way beamed wide,
Stars winked, not a frown in sight!
With laughter echoing afar,
A universe full of bizarre!

Intergalactic Ironies

A star said, 'I'm feeling blue,'
'Guess I'm too far from you!'
Laughter echoed through the throng,
While planets hummed a joyful song.

A moon cheered, 'Let's launch a show!'
'The sun can't stand the glow!'
They twinkled bright, causing a fuss,
With cosmic giggles, oh, what a plus!

Black holes opened, sucked in the puns,
'They're stellar, but still way fun!'
Nebulae puffed in shades so neat,
As they danced to a galactic beat.

In this cosmic fair of jest,
Every rival star knew best.
With irony spun 'round and 'round,
The universe found humor profound!

Witty Wormholes

Wormholes twist and shout with flair,
'Strike a pose, if you dare!'
Through these loops, galaxies peek,
Their jokes hide, seek and sneak.

One said, 'I'll give you a ride,
But hold on tight, it's a bumpy slide!'
Warping time with every jest,
A cosmic spin, the universe's fest.

Stars teamed to launch a pun fair,
'Let's play tag, catch me if you care!'
They zipped and zoomed with such delight,
Creating laughter through the night.

Across the void, smiles were shared,
Every supernova prepared.
Witty tales in the cosmic breeze,
Floating laughter through the galaxies.

Jovian Jokes

Jupiter laughed with a booming sound,
'Got any jokes that astound?'
His moons lined up in a playful row,
Throwing puns like a cosmic show.

Saturn chimed in, rings in full sway,
'Why did the rocket refuse to play?'
'Because it felt a bit too spaced!'
And with that, the laughter raced.

The gas giants spun with cheer,
Filling the void with cosmic jeer.
Their laughter rocked the scenes so bright,
With jovial jests lighting the night.

And as they glimmered, shining bold,
Each story was a gem untold.
Their humor danced, a celestial rhyme,
In the vastness, love for all time!

www.ingramcontent.com/pod-product-compliance
Lightning Source LLC
Chambersburg PA
CBHW071845160426
43209CB00003B/417